The Shawnee

by Petra Press

Content Adviser: Dr. Bruce Bernstein, Assistant Director for Cultural Resources, National Museum of the American Indian, Smithsonian Institution

Social Science Adviser: Professor Sherry L. Field, Department of Curriculum and Instruction, College of Education, The University of Texas at Austin

Reading Adviser: Dr. Linda D. Labbo, Department of Reading Education, College of Education, The University of Georgia

 COMPASS POINT BOOKS

Minneapolis, Minnesota

Compass Point Books
3722 West 50th Street, #115
Minneapolis, MN 55410

Visit Compass Point Books on the Internet at *www.compasspointbooks.com* or e-mail your request to *custserv@compasspointbooks.com*

Cover: Cover: Shawnee John Gibson in clothing with large feather bustles at the Red Earth Festival in Oklahoma City, Oklahoma

Photographs ©: David & Peter Turnley/Corbis, cover, 16; Kit Breen, 4, 14; David Muench/Corbis, 7; North Wind Picture Archives, 8, 9, 11, 21, 24–25, 26, 27, 28–29; Ben Klaffke, 10, 40, 42; Unicorn Stock Photos/Jeff Greenberg, 12; Marilyn "Angel" Wynn, 13, 30; Maass/Corbis, 15; Nancy Carter/North Wind Picture Archives, 15, 34; Hulton Getty/Archive Photos, 17, 19, 33, 37, 38; Marc Muench/ Corbis, 22; National Museum of American Art, Washington DC/Art Resource, NY, 31; G. E. Kidder Smith/Corbis, 36; AP/Wide World Photos/Michael Heinz, 41.

Editors: E. Russell Primm, Emily J. Dolbear, and Alice K. Flanagan
Photo Researchers: Svetlana Zhurkina and Jo Miller
Photo Selector: Catherine Neitge
Designer: Bradfordesign, Inc.
Cartographer: XNR Productions, Inc.

Library of Congress Cataloging-in-Publication Data
Press, Petra.
    The Shawnee / by Petra Press.
        p. cm. — (First reports)
    Includes bibliographical references and index.
    ISBN 0-7565-0188-1
    1. Shawnee Indians—Juvenile literature. [1. Shawnee Indians. 2. Indians of North America—East (U.S.)] I. Title. II. Series.
E99.S35 P74 2002
974.004'973—dc21   2001004415

Table of Contents

▲ *George White Cloud Sullivan at a Shawnee dance*

People on the Move

Long ago, the Shawnee people lived in the north-eastern United States. The Shawnee people moved so often, no one knows for sure where their first villages were. Over thousands of years, the Shawnee may have traveled as far north as Canada and as far south as Florida.

The Shawnee often lived with other Indian tribes. From time to time, they shared the forests with Delaware, Fox, Kickapoo, and Cheyenne tribes. Many Shawnee lived along the Ohio River in what is now the state of Ohio.

The Shawnee often split up to form new groups. Some joined the other tribes they already lived with. Others traveled to new places.

Europeans began to settle in North America in the late 1600s. By that time, many Shawnee lived in the southern United States.

Legend

- Early Shawnee homelands
- ✸ Battle site
- • Present-day tribal headquarters

0 — 100 miles
0 — 100 kilometers

Lake Huron

Lake Michigan

Lake Ontario

Lake Erie

Wisconsin

Michigan

New York

Iowa

UNITED STATES

Nebr.

Battle of Fallen Timbers, 1794

Ohio

Pa.

Mississippi

Missouri

Illinois

United Remnant Band (headquarters in Urbana, Ohio)

Indiana

Kansas

Missouri

W. Va.

Loyal Shawnee Tribe of Oklahoma (headquarters in White Oak, Okla.)

Eastern Shawnee Tribe of Oklahoma (headquarters in Seneca, Mo.)

Ohio

Kentucky

Virginia

Oklahoma

Absentee Shawnee Tribe (headquarters in Shawnee, Okla.)

North Carolina

Arkansas

Tennessee

South Carolina

Mississippi

Ala.

Georgia

N
W + E
S

La.

ATLANTIC OCEAN

Florida

▲ Shawnee homelands and tribal headquarters

▲ *Many years ago the Shawnee lived along the Ohio River.*

The name *Shawnee* comes from two Shawnee words. One is *shawan*, which means "south." The other is *shawunogi*, which means "southerners." The Shawnee also call themselves *Shawano*.

Today, most Shawnee live in Oklahoma, Missouri, and Ohio. They belong to one of four separate **bands**. They are Absentee Shawnee, Eastern Shawnee, Loyal Shawnee, and United Remnant.

A Shawnee Village

In earlier times, the Shawnee lived in houses called wigiwas. These houses were made of bent tree poles. They were covered with bark or animal furs.

In summer, the Shawnee built a long wigiwa with an arched roof. In winter, they built a round wigiwa. Much later, the Shawnee lived in log cabins.

▲ *The Shawnee lived in houses made of bent tree poles covered with bark or furs.*

Many wigiwas made up a village. The Shawnee built a tall fence around each village. This fence of sharpened tree poles was called a **palisade**.

The people grew crops outside the palisade. They grew corn, beans, pumpkins, sweet potatoes, tobacco, and squash. They also gathered wild plants, such as onions and berries. Children learned by helping the adults.

▲ *Everyone helped harvest the corn.*

▲ *Traditional Shawnee moccasins*

Shawnee women made the clothing and shoes, or moccasins. They prepared the meals and raised the children. They were in charge of the village when the men left to hunt.

Shawnee men hunted buffalo, deer, turkey, and panthers. They used bows and arrows, stone knives, and wooden clubs. They also set traps for foxes, rabbits, raccoons, and beavers.

Animals were more than food for the Shawnee. The Shawnee traded animal skins and furs with white traders and other Native Americans. In return, they got coffee, wool blankets, metal cooking pans, and glass beads. Later, they traded for guns and horses.

▲ *Many Native American tribes used bows and arrows to hunt.*

Community Life

Family and community have always been very important to Shawnee people. Grandparents, aunts, uncles, and cousins all lived near one another.

Families are part of **clans**. Each clan has an animal name. The spirit of this animal guides and protects the clan. Some clan names are Snake, Hawk, Deer, Bear, Wolf, Elk, and Buffalo.

▲ *One Shawnee clan is named after the deer.*

Every newborn baby is given a personal name and a clan name. For example, a child born into the Horse clan might be given the name Spotted Horse.

Summer was a busy time for the Shawnee. People tended crops, hunted, and gathered food. It was also a time for fun. People got together to celebrate family and special events.

Many gatherings were held in the village's **council house**. Near the council house, the Shawnee held dances every year.

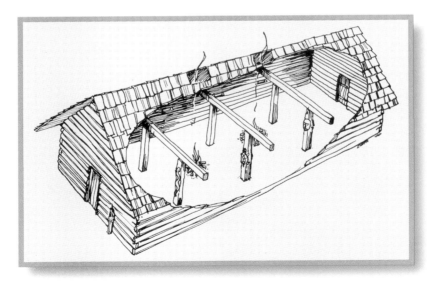

▲ *Many Shawnee gatherings were held in a large council house.*

▲ *A traditional Shawnee dance*

At the Spring Bread Dance, the Shawnee prayed for good crops. They honored the village women who grew and prepared food for the tribe. Men and women also played a ball game to bring rain. Then they planted the first crop of corn.

▲ *The Shawnee celebrated a good corn crop.*

▲ *Shawnee John Gibson at a celebration in Oklahoma City*

At the Green Corn Dance, people celebrated the growing corn. They gave thanks for the new crop.

In the fall, the Shawnee held another Bread Dance. They honored the hunters and gave thanks for a good hunt. Today, the Shawnee still hold these dances in the spring and fall.

Peace and War Chiefs

▲ *Kishkalwa was a Shawnee chief and warrior.*

Each Shawnee village had two main leaders, or chiefs. Shawnee villages had a peace chief and a war chief. These chiefs were usually men.

The peace chief was in charge of village activities except farming. He often passed the job on to his son.

The war chief had to have bravery, skill, and

experience. After a peace chief decided to go to war, the war chief took control of the village. He made all the important decisions.

A female leader was in charge of farming in Shawnee villages. She was called Principal Woman. Often this woman was the chief's wife.

Women could also become chiefs. They were often related to male chiefs. After a chief died, his sister or wife might take over. Female chiefs were known for their bravery, skill, and experience, too.

Teenage girls were not trained for war as well as boys were. However, they often fought alongside boys in battles.

Shawnee Religion

▲ *Hayne Hudjihini, or the Eagle of Delight, was a respected Shawnee woman.*

The Shawnee respect for women comes from their religion. They believe that God, or the Creator, is a woman. They call her "Our Grandmother," or Kohkumthena (go-goom-THA-na). Her home is in the sky.

The Shawnee believe that Kohkumthena created the first people long ago. She gave them rules to live by.

According to the Shawnee, Kohkumthena watches them to see if they are following these rules. During the day, Kohkumthena weaves a net. A dog lies by her side. Every night the dog takes her weaving apart. Every morning Kohkumthena begins again.

One day, Kohkumthena will finish her work. On that day, the world will come to an end.

Kohkumthena will gather everyone into her net. She will keep those who have been good and throw out those who have been evil. Then Kohkumthena will make a new world for the good people she has saved.

The Shawnee believe that Kohkumthena made spirits to help people follow her rules. The spirits live in everything—even in rocks, rivers, and stars. The spirits protect and guide people. Evil spirits cause sickness and accidents.

Shawnee healers are called **shamans**. They treat the sick and wounded with prayers and special **herbs**. They ask the good spirits to help them cure the sick.

▲ *Shamans treated the sick with prayers and special herbs.*

Trading and War

▲ *The Shawnee met Europeans for the first time in what we now call Tennessee.*

European explorers and traders met the Shawnee for the first time around 1670. They were traveling through what is now Tennessee and North Carolina.

The Spanish had come north from Florida. The English and the French had moved from the east coast.

At first, the Shawnee and the Europeans were friendly and traded together. The explorers asked Shawnee hunters to guide them across their lands.

Some traders even married Shawnee women. They followed the Shawnee way of life.

The traders moved with the Shawnee when they returned to the Ohio River valley in the 1700s. Then things changed. Europeans began to fight one another for the land.

In 1754, war broke out between France and Great Britain. Many Native Americans fought in that war. Most Shawnee fought with the French. The war was called the French and Indian War.

Britain won the war in 1763. After the war, settlers burned down Shawnee villages and took the Shawnee land.

War broke out again in 1775. This time the settlers were fighting British soldiers. They no longer wanted to be ruled by Britain. Instead, they wanted to run their own country. The war was called the American Revolution.

▲ *The Shawnee fought with the British in the American Revolution.*

In this war, the Shawnee fought with the British troops. The Shawnee were led to believe that Britain would help stop the flow of settlers onto their land.

But Britain lost the war in 1783. Once again, settlers flooded into Native American lands.

Fallen Timbers

▲ *General "Mad Anthony" Wayne and his troops fought the Shawnee at Fallen Timbers in Ohio.*

The Shawnee continued to defend their land and way of life. They attacked settlers who crossed the Ohio River. The U.S. government sent soldiers to protect the settlers.

By the late 1700s, the Shawnee had fought many battles against U.S. soldiers. At first, the Shawnee were well organized. They won their battles against the U.S. troops.

In 1794, the Shawnee lost an important battle at Fallen Timbers in Toledo, Ohio. Then for an entire year, U.S. general "Mad Anthony" Wayne and his troops burned down Shawnee villages.

▲ *U.S. soldiers destroyed Native American villages.*

After their loss at Fallen Timbers, the Shawnee chiefs stopped fighting. On August 3, 1795, they signed a **treaty** with the U.S. government. It was called the Greenville Treaty.

In the treaty, the Shawnee people agreed to give up most of their land in Ohio and a large part of Indiana. The land covered more than 25,000 square miles (64,750 square kilometers). In return, the U.S. government promised to give the Shawnee $20,000 in supplies. The government also promised to give the

▲ *Native Americans on the Ohio River*

Shawnee $9,500 in supplies each year after that. The government forced these Shawnee to move from the Ohio River valley to Indian Territory, now known as Oklahoma and Kansas.

The Brave Tecumseh

▲ *Tecumseh*

One young Shawnee chief would not sign the Greenville Treaty. This chief's name was Tecumseh (tih-KUHM-suh). He believed that Indian lands belonged to all Native Americans. He said that one tribe alone could not give away land.

Tecumseh set out to bring together all the tribes. His goal was to make the Ohio River a dividing line between the Native Americans and the white settlers.

▲ *Tenskwatawa, as painted by famous frontier artist George Catlin*

Tecumseh had a brother named Tenskwatawa. He was known as the Shawnee Prophet. Tenskwatawa supported his brother's ideas.

In 1808, the two brothers established a town called Tippecanoe in Indiana Territory. Many Native Americans came to live there.

Tenskwatawa told the people to return to their old way of life. He told them to give up what they had learned from the settlers. Then, he told them, they would get back their land and white people would disappear forever.

Tecumseh visited every tribe from Florida to the head of the Missouri River. He asked the tribes to join him in his fight to protect the Native American home-lands.

The British saw Tecumseh bringing the tribes together. The British asked for his help in their new war with the Americans.

Tecumseh agreed. He thought if the British won the war, Americans would be forced to leave Indian lands.

In 1812, the British made Tecumseh a general in their army. They gave weapons to all the friendly tribes.

The Shawnee fought bravely. Tecumseh led them well. In 1813, Tecumseh was killed in a battle near the Thames River in Ontario, Canada.

▲ *Tecumseh was killed in 1813 during a battle near the Thames River in Ontario.*

Today, the people of Canada honor Tecumseh as a hero. The battlefield where he died has been made into a park.

▲ *A statue of Tecumseh in Annapolis, Maryland*

Leaving a Homeland

After Tecumseh died, the Shawnee in the Ohio Valley lost their will to fight. After the war, some went to live with Shawnee who had moved to Missouri and Illinois. Others went to live in Kansas and Texas.

In 1830, the U.S. government passed a law. This law forced all Native Americans in the eastern United States to live in Indian Territory west of the Mississippi River. Over 60,000 Native Americans made this long journey to what is now Oklahoma and Kansas.

Living in Oklahoma was hard. The land was difficult to farm. There were few animals to hunt. The U.S. government gave out food, but it was not enough. People died of disease and hunger.

The government forced Native Americans to change their way of life. They had to give up their language, religion, and customs. Young children were taken from their families and sent away to schools.

▲ *In the mid-1800s, Indian children from many tribes were sent to the Shawnee Methodist Mission School near Kansas City.*

Oklahoma Territory did not belong to the Indians forever. During the mid-1800s, more and more white settlers crossed the Mississippi River and headed west. They settled wherever they wanted.

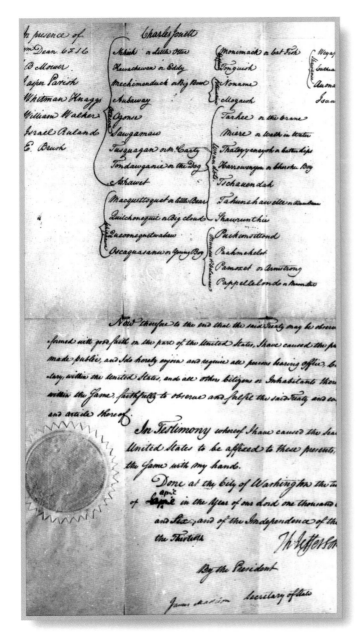

In 1887, the U.S. government passed a law that divided Indian Territory. This law gave each tribe a piece of land. It was a change for the Native Americans. In the past, they had taken care of the land rather than owned it.

◄ *Many treaties were signed with the Shawnee and other tribes, including this one from the early nineteenth century bearing President Thomas Jefferson's signature.*

The rest of the land was given to white settlers. It was millions of acres. In 1889, 50,000 white settlers raced across the border to get their land.

Few Shawnee could make a living on the small plot of land in Oklahoma. Many had to sell their land at low prices just to survive.

▲ Settlers rushed to get land in the Oklahoma Territory in 1889.

The Shawnee Today

Today, four bands of Indians make up the Shawnee Nation. Each band has its own building where it handles tribal business.

The Loyal Shawnee Tribe of Oklahoma is the largest band. Its members are related to the Shawnee who were loyal to the Union during the American Civil War. This Shawnee band has a tribal building in White Oak, Oklahoma.

The Eastern Shawnee Tribe of Oklahoma has its tribal offices in Seneca, Missouri. Every year the tribe holds **powwows** with dance contests for members of all ages.

The Absentee Shawnee of Oklahoma are related to the Shawnee who were gone when the land was divided. This Shawnee band's offices are in Shawnee, Oklahoma.

▲ *Shawnee tribal land in Oklahoma*

The Shawnee Nation United Remnant Band moved to Tecumseh's homeland in Ohio from Indiana in 1971. Its offices are in Urbana, Ohio. The U.S. government does not yet recognize this group as Shawnee people.

In the 1990s, about 6,000 Shawnee living in Oklahoma were listed as tribal members. Today, some live on **reservation** land. Most live on private land.

▲ *Hawk Pope is chief of the Shawnee Nation United Remnant Band.*

▲ These children are members of the Absentee Shawnee band.

Some Shawnee people work as ranchers, farmers, and business owners. Others work as doctors, nurses, lawyers, teachers, writers, artists, and musicians.

Over the years, the Shawnee Nation has experienced many changes. Most changes were forced on them.

Today, the Shawnee are making their own decisions. Most Shawnee live like other Americans. Yet some things make the Shawnee different from other Americans. Their history, language, and beliefs are special.

The Shawnee people continue to work hard to hold on to their way of life. That way of life lives on in the wisdom of the elders and the promise of the children.

Glossary

bands—groups of people who live and travel together

clans—groups of related families

council house—the meeting place for a tribal group chosen to make important decisions

herbs—healing plants

palisade—a fence made of sharpened tree poles

powwows—Native American ceremonies with feasting and dancing

reservations—large areas of land set aside for Native Americans; in Canada, reservations are called reserves

shamans—leaders of ceremonies to heal people or to honor the spirits of the dead

treaty—an agreement between two governments

- *Tecumseh* means "shooting star" or "meteor." *Tenskwatawa* means "the open door."

- Frontiersman and explorer Daniel Boone lived with the Shawnee for three months. The Shawnee took Boone and members of his hunting party as prisoners in 1778.

- In the past, Shawnee men and women played a form of football with a buckskin ball filled with deer hair.

- Shawnee women sewed European glass beads on their leather clothing and moccasins.

At a Glance

Tribal name: Shawano

Divisions: Absentee Shawnee, Eastern Shawnee, Loyal Shawnee, and United Remnant

Past locations: Ohio, Indiana, Illinois, Pennsylvania, Maryland, Virginia, Tennessee, Missouri, Kansas, Kentucky, Alabama, Georgia, North Carolina, Florida, Texas, Canada

Present locations: Oklahoma, Ohio, Missouri, Canada

Traditional houses: Wigiwas, log cabins

Traditional clothing materials: Skins, cotton, wool

Traditional transportation: Horses

Traditional food: Wild plants, fish, buffalo, deer, turkey, panthers

Important Dates

1670s	European explorers and traders arrive in Shawnee lands.
1754– 1763	The Shawnee fight with the French in the French and Indian War.
1775– 1783	The Shawnee fight with the British in the American Revolution.
1794	The Shawnee lose a battle at Fallen Timbers in Toledo, Ohio.
1795	The Shawnee sign the Greenville Treaty.
1808	Tecumseh and his brother establish a town called Tippecanoe in Indiana Territory.
1812	The British make Tecumseh a general in their army.
1813	Tecumseh is killed in a battle near the Thames River in Ontario, Canada.
1830	The U.S. Congress passes the Indian Removal Act, which forces Indians onto reservations.
1924	The Shawnee are granted U.S. citizenship.
1971	The Shawnee Nation United Remnant Band moves to Tecumseh's homeland in Ohio.

Want to Know More?

At the Library

Cwiklik, Robert. *Tecumseh: Shawnee Rebel.* New York: Chelsea House Publishers, 1992.

Flanagan, Alice. *The Shawnee.* Danbury, Conn.: Children's Press, 1998.

Immell, Myra. *Tecumseh.* San Diego, Calif.: Lucent Books, 1997.

On the Web

Eastern Shawnee Tribe of Oklahoma
http://showcase.netins.net/web/shawnee/history/history.html
For more information about tribal government, traditions, and history

Ohio History Central: Shawnee Indians
http://www.ohiokids.org/ohc/history/h_indian/tribes/shawnee.html
For more information about Shawnee traditions, history, and lifestyle

Through the Mail

Ohio Historical Society
1982 Velma Avenue
Columbus, OH 43211
To learn more about the Shawnee and other Native Americans in Ohio

On the Road

Zane Shawnee Caverns
at the Shawnee and Woodland Native American Museum
7092 State Route 540
Bellefontaine, OH 43311
937/592-9592
To see Native American lands and learn about Shawnee history

Index

About the Author

Petra Press is a freelance writer of young adult non-fiction, specializing in the diverse culture of the Americas. Her more than twenty books include histories of U.S. immigration, education, and settlement of the West, as well as portraits of numerous original cultures. She lives with her husband, David, in Milwaukee, Wisconsin.

48